# HOW TO: SURF IN YOUR 40'S

### BY DANIEL KANAAN

© Daniel Kanaan

Dedicated to my wife, who has helped me in more ways than I can count, and my kids who make my life complete.

# PROLOGUE

It's 2020, infamous for the Coronavirus pandemic, but instead of hunkering down, I took my family to Hawaii and learned to surf. This book documents that journey and will inspire you to let loose, catch a wave, and go with a flow.

# 1.
# GO IN OVER YOUR HEAD

I rented a movie star house on the North Shore of Oahu, Hawaii. Coronavirus is sweeping the world, shutting down business, killing people, and propelling the stock market to new heights. A lot of life is completely irrational. The stock market is irrational. Shutting down outdoor beaches is irrational. But in the heart, we know what the right thing to do is. And the right thing to do back in July of 2020 was take the family for an indefinite vacation in Hawaii. Let me explain.

I suffer from anxiety to a degree that makes me look extremely relaxed. And 2020 presented the following, in no particular order. To start the year, myself and my daughter both caught a fairly low grade cough. We had just eaten dinner at my friends house, and he was recovering from a nasty cold of some kind. He'd been traveling to the UK at the time. Then the news presented us with a new disease, Covid-19. Stock market tanks. Everyone is scared. I make a social media post saying that the fear and reaction to the disease is worse than the disease itself. Some of my friends take offense. So I get off social media.

Social media is a serious problem. It has provided some benefit, but on the whole, it creates the perfect storm for fear induced hysteria, very similar to what Covid-19 does to the body. The overreaction of the body is worse than the disease. The overreaction to this disease is worse than the disease.

So I wasn't falling for it. After a big fight with my wife, and then a big night drinking at my friends house, I decided in my hung-over state, to book a month long trip to Hawaii, with the idea of extending it once we got there. At the time, Hawaii was forcing travelers to stay in their house for two weeks. No Beach. Come on. Really? Since the risk of outdoor transmission of any virus is nil, the quarantine was an overreach. Hawaii should have applied the same rules (no indoor gathering without ventilation) to everybody. They would have had a tourist industry. My plan was to go to and simply ignore the quarantine, at least as far as beaches went. Which is what we did.

Unfortunately we had an Airbnb host that lied about her listing, and we found out when we got there that she was living in the same house. We immediately moved places and asked for a refund, but the damage was done. She watched us like a hawk and reported us to a vigilante group that made it its mission to spy on quarantine breakers. It was only a matter of time before we were caught and then arrested. Not fun.

So what does this have to do with surfing? Well, just about everything, actually. By doing something extraordinary: traveling to Hawaii in the middle of a pandemic while planning on breaking the law, we were in over our head. Getting arrested and mug-shotted was the equivalent of getting out into the water and suddenly realizing that the waves are MUCH BIGGER in person.

But that doesn't mean you shouldn't go out there. This morning, I went out into the waves outside my North Shore oceanfront place for the first time. The waves were smaller than yesterday. I was with my friend (who's a little more experienced than I). And together we decided to go out and do it, regardless.

When we got out there, the waves were crazy big. We were on lousy Costco foam surf boards, lousy only for the conditions, not generally lousy. We didn't have a clue what we were doing. My friend's leash was barely holding on. But there we were, out in the ocean looking at some monster waves.

I got rolled over and broken on, but I'm a good swimmer, and I have a lot of breath. Then I almost caught another wave, but the nose went in and I got rolled again. I got my board and went towards the next wave that was breaking and I got rolled again. And now I was adrenalin shooting. So I caught the next white water and just lay down while it took me in, over a reef that tagged my fins. I made it to the deeper water and turned to go home. I hoped my friend would see me, but I wasn't sure so I just tried to get back to the launch site in front of my house and signal to him.

When I got there and turned and saw him following me. Once he got in, he told me, "The leash just popped off and the board went in. I had to chase it." The reef was the same I had scraped my fin on, but he was all cut up on his knees and toes.

But we're still alive. We'll be heading back to the beginners beach later, but the point is, what we did, going in over our head, needed to be done. We learned that fear was not our master, and that going in over your head is something that HAS TO BE DONE if you want to live a full life. So I urge you: if you want to surf, start going in over your head. Who knows? You might end up in Hawaii with a million bucks.

# 2.
# MAKE A MILLION BUCKS

The reason I'm sitting in a multi-million dollar house on the waters off the north shore are many. Covid has decimated the tourism in Hawaii. Hawaii has decimated the tourism in Hawaii by passing laws that prevent rental under thirty days unless you're a ~~political donor~~ licensed dwelling. This perfect storm means that a house that normally costs $1000 a night, is renting for $12,000 a month. Sure that's still a fair chunk, but this is a $4 million dollar house on the water in the North Shore of Oahu, so $12,000 is less than the mortgage payment. That's why this house is for sale.

But the reason I'm willing to blow $12,000 a month in Hawaii for that last three months is because I made a million bucks in the stock market and now I'm going to do nothing but sit here and write this book about how to surf through your forties. I lost my job in May. It payed

$200,000 per year. So I just netted five years salary and I'm going to enjoy the next five years. And I'm learning to surf. And I'm never going back to the person that I was before I made a million bucks.

But that doesn't mean YOU have to make a million bucks. Because more likely than not, YOU are MUCH HEALTHIER than I was. Psychologically. Because you see, I was raised to believe that you needed money in order to do what you want. When in fact YOU DON'T NEED MONEY TO DO WHAT YOU WANT.

You heard me right. I'm almost positive that my fellow surfers out here haven't made a million bucks. They are way better surfers than me, particular the ones I saw this morning. Why has it taken me so long to start surfing? Because I lived under the illusion that a million dollars was required in order to start living the life you love. And for me, it might be true because I have always had the idea that I'm a fucking loser and that having money was the proof that you were winning.

But it isn't true. Sure money is great. Make a million bucks if you can, but don't sweat it if it isn't up your street. A million bucks nowadays will barely buy you out of a health crisis. In fact, most people (most likely including myself) will not be able to retire on a million bucks because old age in America is incredibly expensive. Health care is not free and you will end up blowing your wad on medical bills.

So stop thinking like that. Be poor if you can't help it. You don't need to feed the economic system. Feeding the economic system is equivalent to fear, because you are really just afraid to go out of your comfort zone of a nice house in the suburbs with "good schools." People who realize that this is a trap do one of two things: they abandon the idea of wealth, or they get wealthy. So that is your choice.

When you see a wave coming at you, you have a choice. You can either swim towards it, or surf. Because if you do nothing, you are going to get rolled. Making the decision to demand more from life is equivalent to doing nothing. Sure you won't die, but you won't really live either. Moving towards the wave is an abandonment, and a way of saving energy. But surfing the wave, is the way of life, the way forward. Start small, but whatever you do: start surfing.

# 3.
# IF YOU'RE ALONE, YOU'RE DOING IT WRONG

When you go out into the waves, there will be a few "groups" of people. Those farther out are looking for the bigger waves. The biggest waves break the farthest out. On a particular day, the closest group of surfers to the shore are waiting for smaller breaks, and they'll be protected from getting broken upon by the big waves, even though they will be fighting a little more white water than those who are all the way out. The farthest out won't really have any fighting to do, so they can pretty much relax, unless, of course, they are just a little too far "in" (closer to shore), in which case the biggest waves can pose a danger to them.

This is pretty much where you don't want to be. If you look at the groups of surfers, you should really just pick one, rather than being "alone" somewhere. Why? Because if you're in the middle somewhere, you'll be in the way of the farthest group, you'll catch a lot of white water, and you won't really find many great waves.

In my life, I've tried to do things on my own, and I haven't ever really succeeded at them. This makes me think I'm in the wrong place. As an artist, I've almost always ended up in the middle. And I find myself not really catching any kind of waves. But I'm tired of that. I want to go and join the groups.

I've always thought that if you're alone, you're either a genius or an idiot. I think I'm beginning to finally realize that, actually, you're more than likely just an idiot. If I start to think about people I envy for success, they are always part of a group. The idea that I'm so great, so awesome, that I simply can't be recognized by anyone until it's too late, is this strange one that I've been carrying around for decades. The "you just don't get it" thing is getting really stale.

That's why I'm giving up on being an artist. There just isn't any action there. So I'm looking toward the groups. I'm rejoining society, losing my arrogance, and following the groups to catch the waves.

# 4.
# THE BEST WAVES ARE THE ONES YOU CAN CATCH

You can look at almost anything abstractly. If I watch the ocean from my lanai, the waves are abstract. But when I'm in the water, the waves become very real very quickly.

When I went out in the craziness of Outer Alligators and got tossed around, it wasn't fun. It served a purpose because most waves now seem pretty small. I'm always tempted to push myself. Push push push push. Its fucking exhausting. Going to Outer Alligators was a push, a challenge. The hardest thing I have ever done was downgrading my ambition. I've learned that relaxing, being relaxed, is the hardest thing to do.

I look at the achievement of others and I think, wouldn't it be great to be there. Just like looking at these surfers out on the big breaks and thinking, wouldn't it be great to be there. But to GET there, you have to go somewhere else entirely, somewhere where the abstract can be realized.

Ride the waves you enjoy. People say "no pain no gain" but they are wrong. You can only progress if you are roughly within your comfort zone. Sure treat yourself to a little challenge, but make it like ten percent or so. The majority of your time should be spent enjoying whatever skills you have and not trying to do the next great thing.

I learned to stand up on the surfboard my first day. So I'm going to just keep riding the waves I know will treat me well until I'm bored as fuck. Because that's called enjoyment, and it's something I've been stingy to myself with my whole life. Which goes back to that terrible anxiety. Demanding shit from yourself is the surest way to cruise miserably to an early grave. By all means, if you're talented and achieve greatness with ease and grace, then enjoy that, because chances are you DO enjoy it already. But if surfing a 10 foot wave isn't up your street, then enjoy the 4 foot waves until you don't anymore.

I see many, many days surfing the beginner beaches in my near future. I'm going to enjoy every single one.

# 5.
## USE THE FUN BOARD

When we arrived at this beautiful place, there were, according to the gardener "a couple of Costco surfboards" that were at our disposal. When we arrived I was not considering becoming a surfer, so I really barely acknowledged them.

The first time I went out with my buddy on them, we tried and failed to catch some pretty damn big waves. After 20 minutes being brutalized by those things, we decided to go off to a different area with a shallow reef near shore. I got rolled hard and just rode the white water in, scraping my board on the reef. I turned to see if he'd made it in, and he was behind me. As he arrived he told me his leash had snapped off and he lost his board. He got all cut up on that shallow reef before he could get his board again. He blamed the "foamies" as he called them. Then he said if he had a leash, he'd try again in slightly calmer conditions.

I nodded in agreement, suddenly feeling that the surfboards that the great god had handed up were somehow not up the job. We talked about how "floppy" they were and how they didn't have any edges. We looked at all the surfers out there with "real boards."

And then, yesterday evening, a local Hawaiian appeared in some pretty large waves, albeit pretty clean. He paddled out near our house.

"He's on a foamy," I said to my friend

"Really?" He replied. "Well, let's see how he does."

We watched him paddle out towards the right side, "Uppers" it's called, where the really big waves were. I grabbed the binoculars and sat and waited to see what would happen. There were a group of five or so out there already and he seemed right at home. Then, in the distance, I see a giant coming in.

"Alright, let's see what he does."

Sure enough he caught it beautifully. Through the binoculars I watched his absolute calm as he glided his hand through the green wall of water. He passed the white water and came back up over the top of the wave.

"Wow." I said. "He did alright. I guess it's not the board."

We watched him catch a few more waves, equally gracefully. And then he started his paddle home. I followed him all way in. As he pulled his "foamy" out of the water, I made the final remarkable discovery: no leash.

You see, when you're picking out surfboards, you're going to be presented with a whole of lot expertise about which board is the "right" board. But I'm going to tell you a couple of things. There's a board that's called the "fun board" and that's probably the one you want, because all things being equal, it will probably be the most fun.

# 6.
# FIRST SOLO WAVE

I finally drummed up the nerve to head out to the break right in front of my place. The break is called Outer Alligators and at least two famous surfers have lost their lives in the big break.

No, I didn't wander out into 30 foot waves. In fact, it's the tail end of a week of waves that hit double overhead at this very break. But now, the only waves breaking out there are the overhead waves, and fortunately for me, they are breaking only every several minutes.

The main problem with Alligators is that there is a very shallow reef and if you don't get off the wave, you are liable to hit it. If you plan to fall off your board, then you have to do it before that reef otherwise you get scratched up. So it's a balance between keeping well away from that reef and trying to stay inside the break.

I'm calling it a solo wave because there were no other surfers out there. There were a couple in "Uppers" which is to my right, and several over in "Chun's reef" but none on alligators.

I'm not going to lie I went through just about every excuse in the book. One of my big favorites is "You need to give yourself a break, you see, because you are very sore." Now generally, I know from experience that constant exercise is terrible for your health. But surfing is different because there just aren't always the right waves around so sometimes you have to push through the fatigue. I've been surfing for six straight days, and today is the seventh. Yes, my elbows are sore. So are my shoulders. I really should take a break.

But just look at that! No ones out there. No giant waves to ruin your day. Just the occasional wave that is just big enough to surf. This is my chance. So I take it. I put on the sun screen and head out at 8:30.

As I paddle out, I'm watching. Stopping. Making sure nothing's changing out there. Moving again. Looking for the "right" waves. The biggest of the morning. The ones I can catch, and then jump off before the reef.

As I get to the sweet spot, I look around. Not much. It's a beautiful day. Big puffy clouds in the sky. One of the things I love about Hawaii are the big puffy clouds. There's my place, underneath the sun. I can see the lounge chair where I sit and watch surfers on this very break.  And then a set comes in. I almost get it, but I don't want to go too far in.  I look where they're breaking, which is awfully close to that reef.  I have to bide my time and wait for the biggest of the morning. The worry of the reef is ever present, so I move further out into the calm and wait.

A paddle boarder arrives further in to catch some small waves. Maybe it's high tide and he's not worried about the reef. I'm further out this time. I'm the guy who's waiting for the big waves this time.  The paddle boarder moves off.

Then I see it, my wave. I start paddling and sure enough, I catch it. It's speedy. I move to stand up and then I'm up. I can hear the wave breaking behind me, the turbulence of the white water. I can feel it shoving my board left and right. But I'm riding it. And then I jump off, before the reef, and head back out.

That brief ride is like an awakening consciousness. I imagine it's the way a baby feels when the first lights of memory awaken in the early years. The visions we all still have from childhood. Mine was playing in the garden and my brother getting stung by bees. I must have been 2 or 3 years old.

This ride broke through my mind, all my thoughts and plans, erasing everything and painting a fresh palette of new experience. I had started this day as one person, and became someone else.

When you get a chance, take a risk, go out when no-one is there in a break that only you understand, and ride your first real solo wave.

# 7.
# THE PADDLE BACK

This morning I made a plan to head to Waikiki for the first time to check out a southern swell that was supposed to arrive. I got delayed on an errand for an hour, and was debating whether or not I should bother when I wouldn't arrive before 10am. At that time, the sun is intense, and being out for for an hour or two means that even if you're used to the sun like I am, you will almost certainly still feel some damage.

I decided to go but on the way, about a mile south of my place, I noticed some really nice sized waves on Chun's Reef. I watch Chun's reef from my place through the binoculars and it is a great beginners beach when the surf isn't too crazy. On a day like today, the two breaks outside my house don't break at all, apart from that very shallow reef break at alligators. But Chun's seemed to be breaking just fine, so I turned the car around and headed back to my place to pick up my board and head to Chun's for an hour.

The waves were perfect, and as one experienced boarder pointed out, I had exactly the right board for that day.

"I didn't have much choice," I answered.

"Oh, that's your only board?"

"Yup."

I scanned the waves and noticed two groups of people on the left and the right. But I also noticed that some remnant big waves were coming in farther out right in the center. I paddled out to that and sure enough, every once in several minutes, a big set were come in right down the center.

I caught my first wave with ease, stood up, and then rode the white water all the way until it gave out. What a ride, short and sweet.

I started my paddle back out. The white water was pretty persistent and it took me a solid five minutes or so to get to where I was. That's when I realized how time is affected as you ride the wave. I talked about that expanding consciousness, like a baby waking up to a new thought, but today I was able to feel that out a little better. Riding the wave brings you into a kind of flow that isn't really like anything else. Time takes on a new meaning, and you realize that when you see how far the wave has taken you.

Being a beginner surfer means that the time available to you to "reflect" on the wave is miniscule. Instead, you're paying complete attention to the feel of the board underneath you, the gentle sway to the left and right as you shift your gaze, and the rumble and tug of the white water as it slowly lets off energy. It's only during that paddle back that you realize how far you've actually come.

# 8.
# RELAX

There may be surf every morning but you can't surf every morning. I have more trouble relaxing than anything else. I mean, right now, as I write this, I have a sunburn on my eyeballs, a sore back, sore elbows, sore shoulders, a gash on my ankle, and a toe that does not enjoy walking. My hair is turning blond from the sun. The reason I know I have a sunburn on my eye ball is because when I open my eyes wide, I can see the white part where the eyelid usually covers the cornea, and the red part that's usually open.

So what's the point? Your body needs a break. Being sore is great, being sunburned is fine, but pushing your body to the limits without rest is what eventually ruins your health. How do I know this? Because for last couple of years I got heavily into running, and at one point I was running 4 miles a day, every day. And then eventually my hip started hurting, not badly, but just uncomfortably. So I took a break from exercise only to realize my back was not in a good way.

In fact, what had happened was that the over-running had created a lower back problem, something like Sciatica, but the first symptom was in my hip. That's how it works: when your back is hurting, it actually means you're doing something right. It's called centralization. You want the symptoms to be closer to the problem.

So I had to learn the hard way that even though I could go out and surf at Chun's reef, or even take a drive to Waikiki, where they are having the first biggish surf of the fall, that I probably should take a day where I sit around inside, away from the sun and just stare at my phone all day. With sunglasses.

Taking a rest day puts all the parts of you that are overused to good rest, and it means that when I go out tomorrow morning, when the local surf is expected to be decent. I can expect it to be a lot easier.

Surfing for me has been the symbol of relaxation in a lifetime of anxiety. So for Pete's sake, take a day to regain your strength, ponder the mysteries of life, and do something completely different.

# 9.
# NOW YOU'RE SURFING

Still groggy from sleep, I woke to a lulling surf left over from yesterday's rippers. Yesterday was a great day to take the day off and now I feel like I've woken up not just from a night's sleep but from a week of partying, now fully recovered.

To my right, the waves at uppers are big, but not frightening. Over at alligators, there's already a decent group waiting for the waves. I look off at Chun's reef and I see about 20 or 30 people out where the waves look just about perfect.

I grab my board, load it into the car and head over to Chun's. I park in my usual spot that involves a shaded walk along the sand of a stream outlet, covered in long, dull pine needles. I approach the water and stand looking at the surf. To the right is a smaller group, and the to left, the usual group of long boarders practicing their steps. The waves are just right, so I head out right down the center. I paddle through a few broken waves and then see the largest waves I'll see today. No problem. I paddle past the wave and get out to the calm between the two groups.

My first priority this morning: meditate out there on the ocean. Watch the water and the waves. Take it all in. This is when I really wake up for the day. And then I see a perfect wave. I catch it. Stand up effortlessly and ride it along, watching the reef glide underneath me. I'm moving from left to right, a lot like I used to do on my skateboard as a kid. And when the wave peters out, I get back on the board to paddle back out.

On my first paddle out that morning, I coincided with a group of kids. I kept an eye on them and noticed they were with a couple of adults.

Having caught my first wave, I notice on my paddle back that there are a few adults. I approach the only guy and ask him.

"Is this a school?"

"No," he replies, "You want to join? You look like you could use it."

Now I had just caught a great wave, but I know I must look like a beginner still, so I don't take his comment the wrong way. He catches a wave and disappears. So I head back out to the clear, where I won't be threatened by the largest waves. The kids are waiting for smaller ones, I guess.

After hanging around for a few minutes, I see the same guy again. So I paddle towards him.

"No it was for my kids! I mean I'm a beginner too, but I was really asking for my kids."

So we start a long conversation. We talk about life. He's homeschooling and he has a couple of rentals. He's a carpenter. He's worried about how to teach his kids to make money.

I respond: "I'm more interested in kind of inspiring them, and seeing what they enjoy doing."

We talk about homeschooling, and the group of kids that are all kind of neighbors on the north shore. At this point point, all the kids have gone back in.

During this half hour or so, we're both watching the waves, but we've made a gentleman's agreement to go far out, where we can basically just float on the boards and kind of occasionally pay reverence to the biggest waves of the day.

We get deeper into the conversation, and it takes on a metaphysical quality. This isn't a conversation, it's an encounter of two living beings taking on the biggest questions of life, money, the law, bringing up kids, being married. And all the time, we're being gently reminded that we are out in the middle of almighty nature.

And isn't that what being human is all about? Isn't that what surfing is at its core? Isn't our ability to take the energy of nature and then harness it for joy what separates us from every other animal?

Now you're surfing.

# 10.
# THE SLOW POP, THE SEAL, AND UNCONTROLLABLE JOY

There is so fucking much in the air today I can barely handle it. Our stay in this magnificent house is coming to an end. Sure, I tried to extend, but it was too little, too late. Someone else had already come in and booked it out from under us. On top of that, I have an undeniable feeling that this particular house is responsible for so much of the good that has happened, that I made happen, in my life. I'm certain at this point that the end of our stay here will coincide with a stock market crash, so I've pulled all my stocks into cash. Feels crazy because I'm going to be faced with a ridiculous tax bill, something like a third of a million.

On top of that, we've got nowhere to stay, and the idea of going back to California has me wanting to pull my hair out. I can't face a return to "normality" which for me is just sitting in my house, in my neighborhood, with nothing to do, and more importantly: no surfing. Sure I could surf in California. Pick up a wet suit and freeze my ass off in the frigid California waters. But I know that that will never happen.

With all this weighing on my soul, I head out to Chun's reef on this day that promises no gnarly waves, just gentle rollers asking to be ridden all the way in. I don't know what's going to happen when I get there, but my thoughts are dark, and my body is aching from yesterday. I don't have high hopes.

I scope out the waves and head for my usual spot, off to the right outside the main crown on the left, with a smaller group. Even the biggest of today's wave pose absolutely no threat. Remember: I've been to Alligator Rock, 50/50, and Uppers when the waves were nuts so nothing can scare me.

I catch my first wave, a real beauty, and jerk my way up. Nothing smooth about my pop up, but I've got the wave and the ride feels great. Turn around and head back out. I'm tired after the paddle back so I intentionally move beyond the smaller break where the big waves arrive every ten minutes or so. Out in the distance is a seal, popping its head up and then diving under.

According to the boogie boarder who washed up in front of my house the other day, seals mean no sharks, so I'm happy about that. I relax and peer off towards my house, which I can make out in the distance. It's a gorgeous day, and the water is clean and clear below me.

I spot another wave and it has my name all over it. So I go for it, catch it, and immediately - and this has never happened - I pop right up in one slow but smooth motion. I can feel the board underneath me as the wave lunges us forward and I hang to the left and then just ride it along, making some moves up and down the wave and then feeling the white water push me along.

It's my first smooth pop, and it felt great. Like a baby walking for the first time. Because I hung to left, I'm already near the channel so I work my way back out. There's a group of kids out there and I think maybe my friend my yesterday will show up, but truth be told, I want to solo surf today. I'm not feeling sociable. Nothing to worry about, though because it's a different group.

I catch a few more. My goal is to pop and turn immediately to ride along the wave. The first attempt I pop but I can't convert. Then I miss a few. I've been out here for an hour and a half so I make a decision to go for my last ride. I catch a wave, pop and start moving, but instead of riding it in, I get knocked over. That's not gonna be my last wave, so I start the paddle out.

I'm looking for a smaller wave to break a little inside, so the main group misses it but I catch it. Sure enough, I see one coming. One of the group tries to go, but I see they're gonna miss. I turn my board and start the paddle. When I catch it, I'm right at the top of the wave. I pop up and then drop along the green water and that's when I shout for joy.

The shout came from deep inside my soul, and I let it out as I sped down the wave. That's when I realized that surfing is about a lot of things, but most of all, it's the first time I can remember shouting for joy. As we get older, and in particular as we reach the middle of our lives, we all need a way to shout for joy, because real life is extraordinarily complicated, but the joy of surfing provides the energy that keeps your soul afloat.

# 11.
# EBB AND FLOW

It's a gentle morning on the north shore, I'd say flat, but there are a few swells rolling through uppers beach park. Not breaking, but just rolling through. Surf report says 2-3 feet, poor to fair. I look off towards Chun's reef and I see a dozen or so people sitting on their boards. They're catching some waves, but I think to myself "I'll head to Waimea for some snorkeling."

But this't a book about snorkeling. It's about surfing. And being in your forties. So I head down to Chun's with my board. As I look out over the reef, I see people on the left and on the right and some decent waist high waves coming in, and then periods of flat. So I head out towards the right and take in the scenery.

I know from the forecast that tomorrow will most likely be flat, or certainly almost flat, so this is my last chance until the next swell. As I sit out on my board I think about the waves and their comings and goings, their big days and their inevitable smaller days. In a way, that's just another symbol of our own lives. We start out weak and powerless, and then as we hit our teens, we become incredibly energetic. In our twenties, we mature and become the strongest we will ever be. We can push that strength into our thirties, and Kelly Slater, the famous surfer, won a world tour at 39.

But in our forties, things start to turn. Wounds and bumps take longer to heal. A sore back will most likely just stay that way. "Uncomfortable" one of my good friends calls it. But our forties are relatively powerful compared to our fifties. And so on. Surfing has healed my back and strengthened my core, but it's a hard workout, and I know I will never be like that 12 year old cutting back and forth on the wave, especially once he becomes a man.

But our forties are also a time to reflect on the peak of our lives, what we have accomplished, and what we have failed to accomplish. It's also a great time to sit back and relax and give up and a lot to that stuff that isn't really important. Because if it were important, wouldn't you have done it by now?

The first decent wave comes along and I catch it, feel that rush of green water and then let the white water trundle me forward. I paddle back out.

There are plenty of things I thought I would have achieved. I always thought I'd be a great painter, but that hasn't materialized and I end up feeling betrayed more than anything else. I've watched my ego swell as I prepare a new work, only to deflate as I relegate it to the pile of stuff that sits around, worthless. Every time it happens, it consumes energy, so I am less and less likely to do it again, more and more detached each time it happens.

In our youth, we have so much energy that we end up wasting a ton of it. And it doesn't matter. But in our forties, we have to be wiser, we have to do things that energize us, rather than consume us. And we have to ride that line between worthwhile effort and wasting energy.

Surfing is worthwhile for me because I've found a new source of life, like an infant learning to walk. And on days like today, it's safe, boring even. But you can focus on the waves that you can catch with little effort, and still enjoy the green and white water.

The next wave, I catch and try to turn left, but instead I wipe out. As I paddle back out I ask myself "why am I trying to improve? Why don't I just go with the flow and enjoy every wave?" And that is wisdom. The more you do something, the better you will get at it, so I've learned to stop trying so hard because that is a waste of time and energy. The next wave, I will take it straight in and just enjoy.

I notice that the two groups on the left and right have converged to just one group closer to shore. In this disunited world, we have found unity: everybody taking exactly what is given, sharing it, and enjoying it.

I wait for my last wave, but I miss it. So I go farther in and wait for the smaller ones. I find one right away and enjoy my final ride of the day, a smooth beauty that pushes me almost all the way back.

# 12.
## THE CLOSEOUT

---

This is the end, my friend. All morning as I recover from my Rum binge last night, I have that Doors song running through my head. Always the end. Our time at the Surf House is coming to end, and not by choice. Still, sometimes the Gods speak and we little humans like to think we can just ignore it. I'd like to think I can go on riding these North Shore waves forever, but forever is a long time, and it starts with a winter, for which the North Shore is infamous.

I have a choice to stay at a place by Chun's reef, overlooking the reef and the beach in front of it, or a place near Kawela Bay, which is quieter and has an offshore reef making the near shore calmer and more suitable for swimming than surfing.

I'd love to think I could keep writing these chapters forever, but I know that all rides must come to and, and my time with you is just one such ride. I take out my foamy and put in the trunk, and head out to Chun's. I look off at the waves, which are just starting to get big. Nothing too frightening, but certainly keeping me on my toes big.

I head out to the right, where just a handful of surfers are waiting to peel left. It's funny because it seems like goofy footed surfers (right foot forward), who are in the minority, prefer to peel left. This is similar to snow boarding, where most people simply feel more comfortable "falling" forward rather than backwards. As a snowboarder myself, I have to say, I have no preference so far. On a snow board, you can't just live your whole life turning in one direction. On a surfboard, however, it seems you can. This is why the breaks where you peel right are always more crowded. Roughly 6 to 10 times more crowded, oddly enough. It's almost worth learning to be goofy footed just to enjoy the smaller crowds. Or just enjoy the feeling of falling backwards.

In any case, my first wave is a real thruster and I am slow to pop up so I ride most of the green on my knees. Once I stand, I start moving left towards the channel.

My next ride in, though, is a closeout. The wave moves from great to broken in one moment, rather than peeling. I try to catch it, but the nose of board catches and I fly forward. That's the closeout.

As I sit here recounting the tale, I realize that my story has come to a natural conclusion. If you've read this far, it means you've embarked on a journey that can take you somewhere incredible. I'm looking out from the Surf House and I see the big waves are coming back already. The periods of calm are becoming less frequent. So my days surfing are coming to an end.

If you're the typical person, then you know how short vacations feel. This is no different. But I've made a choice to turn my life into a permanent vacation, but not because I'm going to be sitting around doing nothing. I mean, sure, doing nothing, as it's so famously called, describes most vacations because normally, people are always running around from one errand to another, trying to make ends meet while shuttling their kids between activities.

So vacations often mean doing nothing, and, I have to say: the rest of your life has to start with a period of doing nothing. And then you do something. And me for me that something has been surfing and writing about it.

My next wave is a beauty. I line up the left peel during my paddle, catch the wave and immediately pop up and ride the green. Sure I'm too far back, but this is the first left peel green wave I've ever ridden, and it feels powerful.

I paddle back out and prepare for my last wave of the morning, a short hour long session. I see the perfect little beauty, paddle, catch it, and pop right up, then let the wave take me all the way to the reef.

I'm cutting it short because this is the end of the beginning. I'm going to move up north, away from the intensity of the surf house. Winter is coming, and although I'm going to keep surfing, I'm going to let it go for a while. But remember: you can leave the surf, but the surf will never leave you. Peace out.

# ABOUT THE AUTHOR

Daniel Kanaan grew up around the world and took to surfing in his forties. He has a wife and five kids.

Printed in Great Britain
by Amazon

86592267R00029